4 YEAR STARTER

By
Wendell Patrick Carter

4 YEAR STARTER

By
Wendell Patrick Carter

4 Year Starter
ISBN: 978-1-966480-04-4 Hardbound
Copyright © 2024 by Wendell Patrick Carter

Request for information should be addressed to:
Curry Brothers Marketing and Publishing Group
P.O. Box 247 Haymarket, VA 20168

All rights reserved. No part of this publication may be reproduced, stored in a retrieval system, or transmitted in any form or by any means, electronic, mechanical, photocopy, recording, or any other, except for brief quotations in printed reviews, without the prior permission of the publisher.

Cover Design and Graphics: Vibranium Media Group
Executive Editing: Gerald D. Curry

Introduction

Welcome to 4 Year Starter, a collection of poetry and reflections that chronicles my journey from the gridiron to the page. This book represents more than a recounting of my life—it's a testament to the resilience, faith, and perseverance that shaped my path.

Each poem is a snapshot of a moment, a memory, or a lesson learned. From the challenges of navigating the NFL to the deeper reflections on family, faith, and community, 4 Year Starter is a story told in rhyme, rhythm, and raw honesty. It's a story of triumphs and setbacks, of discovering who I am, and of sharing that discovery with you.

As you read, I hope you'll find yourself walking alongside me—whether it's under the Friday night lights, in the heat of competition, or during quieter moments of introspection. This book is not just my story; it's an invitation for you to reflect on your own journey, your own struggles, and your own victories.

Thank you for taking this journey with me. I hope these words inspire you, challenge you, and remind you that every step—no matter how difficult—has a purpose.

— Wendell Patrick Carter

Table of Contents

Shout Out 1
Wendell / Patricia 2
Believe In You 3
33rd Street 4
10 5
Show Me Your Friends 6
Old Black Men 7
Focus Hill 8
Slouchy N**** 9
Hawaii 10
Newtown Bred 11
Bad Dude 12
Met Michael Jordan 13
Best Athlete 14
Man About A Mule 15
Original Js 16
Against The Grain 17
Get Something From Them 18
Coach Sprague 19
Coach Ward 20
High School All-Star Game 21
4 Year Starter 22
Tracey Sanders 23
Wayne McDuffie 24
Jamie Dukes 25
Brad Scott 26
Bo Jackson 27
Dan McManus 28
Fred Jones 29

Table of Contents

Deion Sanders 30
Bobby Bowden 31
High Brow 32
Mickey Andrews 33
Almost Left 34
Miami Game 35
Melvin Bratton 36
Keith Jackson 37
1988 NFL Draft 38
Lions 1988 Draft Class 39
Pay Her Back 40
Snow Fall 41
You Can't Play 42
LA / ST. Louis Rams 43
California 44
Comedy Act Theatre 45
Goat For The Day 46
Football Camp 47
Jackie Slater 48
Magic Johnson's House 49
Marcus Allen 50
Front Row Seat 51
Kevin Greene 52
Ronnie Lott 53
Chicken and Waffles 54
Terry Crews 55
Game Day 1 56
Chuck Knox 57
Mike Martz 58

Table of Contents

Creature of Habit 59
20 Point Dog 60
Angry At A Blessing 61
Monsters 62
Jerome Bettis 63
Bucs Stadium 64
Sprained my Foot 65
Mind My Business 66
Houston Oilers 67
Welcome to H-Town 68
Houston Celebs 69
Black Cowboys 70
Bruce Matthews 71
DUI 72
Carlos Jones 73
Isaac Bruce 74
Kevin Carter 75
Baptized in the Shower 76
Arizona Cardinals 77
Larry Centers 78
Simon Shanks 79
Tito / Titoya 80
Alcohol isn't Your Friend 81
Mean Joe Green 82
The Program 83
Bro. Lance 84
Sun Devil Stadium 85
Florida Dudes 86
Tight Ends 80s 90s 87

Table of Contents

The Locker Room 88
NFL Coaching 89
Wilbert Montgomery 90
Torry Holt 91
Marshall Faulk 92
Orlando Pace 93
Dan Campbell 94
Calvin Johnson 95
Lomas Brown 96
Tony Wylie 97
Neurofeedback 98
Mental Health 99
Hope They're Proud 100
My Request 101
Planted by God 102

Shout Out

I want to give a shout out

To those that took the doubt out

Back when I ran an out route

You gave me the determination

To be one of the best in the nation

The ones that cheered the progress

And were extremely Happy for my success

To the OGs that looked out

When I could have gotten took out

And the ones that made mistakes

I learned, watched and had some breaks

I even strayed and erred, along my path

But God saved me, from Satan's wrath

He's been so good I must concede

This new gift to make this pen bleed

WENDELL / PATRICIA

MY NAME WENDELL COMES FROM AN UNCLE OF MINE
WHO'S LIFE WAS CUT SHORT, 16 AT THE TIME
13 YEARS LATER, AUNT PATRICIA LEFT THIS EARTH
JUST 1 YEAR BEFORE MY BIRTH
CAN'T IMAGINE LOSING A CHILD
BUT TO LOSE 2 TEENS YRS APART IS WILD
I'VE ALWAYS THOUGHT MY ARRIVAL
AND THEIR BELIEF IN THE BIBLE
GAVE MY GRANDPARENTS THE ABILITY TO COPE
ATLEAST, THAT'S WHAT I HOPE

BELIEVE IN *You*

YOU MUST BE THE 1ST, TO BELIEVE IN YOU
IF YOU DON'T BELIEVE YOURSELF, WHY WOULD OTHERS DO
ASSURE YOURSELF THAT YOU
ARE GOOD AT WHAT YOU DO
YOU KNOW THAT YOU ARE,
ALLOW IT TO SHOW THRU
I ASSURE THAT YOU, WILL RISE UP TO A VIEW
IF YOU HAVE THE CONFIDENCE TO JUST BELIEVE IN YOU

33RD STREET

I grew up on 33rd Street
With both my grandparents, always sweet
The Curry family, I've always liked
Their eldest son Tommy, taught me to ride a bike
Lawrence Jordan was the man, so I wanted to be a star
You ever heard his brother Gene, on that bass guitar
Joanne Manigo spanked me, on the next block over
Broke loose from my grandma, caught next to Grover
Trina and I were the babies for awhile
When the Weeks family passed by, they'd wave and smile
Ms. Baker always walked to the bus
Mr and Mrs. Jackson, never made a fuss
Ms. Sug, some say was rough
I liked her tho, cause she didn't take no stuff
Lil Jerry, was always cool
Mr Freeman was proud of me, when I left for school
Derek, Larry and Amp all came later
1 of those 3 ended up a Gator
But, There's one thing that still remains
Our favorite nursey, Helen Payne
I will tell you again and keep it on repeat
I had a wonderful time on 33rd Street

10

I WAS 10

WHOSE SHOE SIZE, WAS THE SAME BACK THEN

I COULD WEAR THE SAME SHOES, OF GROWN MEN

IT WAS TOUGH, FINDING DRESS SHOES FOR ME

THOSE SHOES FOR ADULTS, WERE UGLY AS CAN BE

I WASN'T ALLOWED TO BE A SLOB

BOUGHT MY OWN CLOTHES, WITH THAT NEW JOB

IN MIDDLE SCHOOL, I GREW, TALL AND LEAN,

MY AGE AND FEET WERE RECONCILED, BY THIRTEEN

BY 12TH GRADE MY FEET GREW SOME MORE

BUT THEY DIDN'T HAVE 14S, IN ANYONE'S STORE

WEARING SMALL SHOES WASN'T FUNNY AT ALL

BUT I NEVER HAD THAT PROBLEM AGAIN , AFTER PRO BALL.

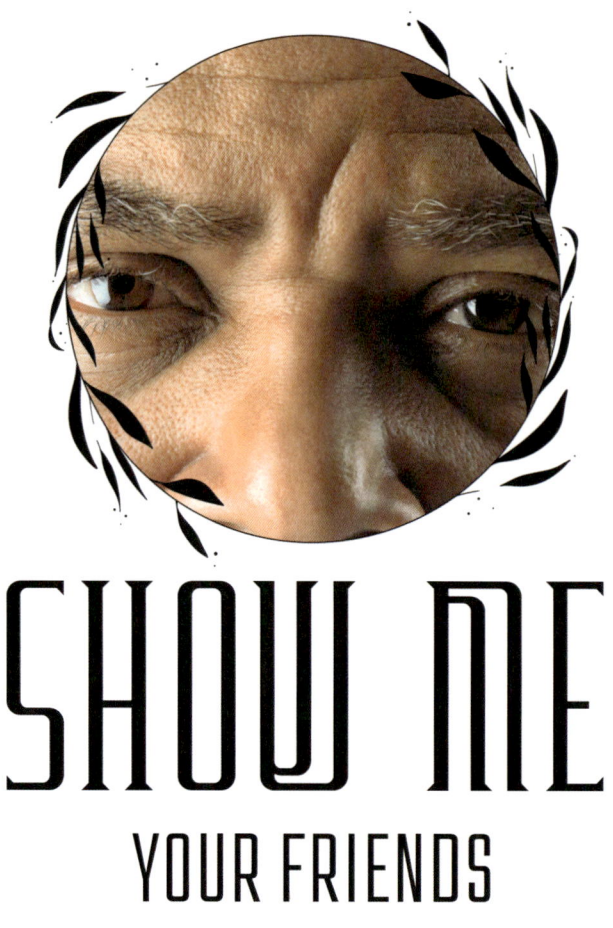

SHOW ME
YOUR FRIENDS

Show me your friends and I'll show you where your headed,
grandma used to say
Never hung with ones who'd disobey
Kept me completely, out of trouble that way
Don't get me wrong, I wasn't a saint
But I was held, mostly in restraint
But squeaky clean, I can't paint
Only the "good boys" I'd acquaint

OLD BLACK MEN

With Old black men I loved to converse
They're the ones that had it worst
Had to step off sidewalks when whites are near
And the threats by the KKK had to strike fear
Paid mere peanuts for excellent work
Folks talking down, face with a smirk
Then they tell of all the lies
Prevents promotions with denies
Seizes folks family land
Then continues to abuse their command
Those old dudes are all gone
I pray They're KNEELING at heaven's throne.

FOOLS HILL

I heard it so relentless, come on grandma chill

Boy change your attitude, you heading up fools hill

My attitude was bitter, pickled like a dill

I was asked to be wiser, temper needed to distill

Often as a teen we don't listen with our ears

Thank goodness I was surrounded by some wiser peers

Never wanted to upset or even disconcert

Work, school and sports kept me on alert

I must admit something that gave such a thrill

I was told I'm proud of you and you're off of fools hill

SLOUCHY
N****

MY GRANDFATHER, I LOVE THAT MAN
ALWAYS WANTED ME TO BE, THE BEST I CAN
SUNDAY MORNINGS WHEN I THOUGHT I WAS DRESSED
GET THAT IRONING BOARD, THAT SHIRT NEEDS TO BE PRESSED
A SLOPPY APPEARANCE COULD REALLY CAUSE A TRIGGER
A WRINKLED SHIRT ON, I HATE A SLOUCHY N****
THAT WAS SOMETHING, I REALLY HATED TO HEAR
SAID IT SO HARSH, DROVE ME TO TEARS

HE NEVER ALLOWED ME TO LEAVE WITH HIM
UNLESS MY APPEARANCE, WAS ALWAYS PRIM
I'M SO THANKFUL FOR WHAT HE DID BACK THEN
APPEARANCE IS IMPORTANT FOR ALL MEN
YEARS LATER AND I'M SO MUCH BIGGER
APPEARANCE NOT PROPER
I HEAR HIS VOICE, SLOUCHY N****.

Hawaii

Former Pres. Obama and I, share a difference from many others
Going to school in Hawaii, we're the only brothers
Schofield Barracks, my dad's work place
We lived with the locals, off the army base
Honowai and neighborhood Loaa St. all cool
Waipahu Intermediate had some racism in their school
Baseball and Hoops are sports I'd play
But I wouldn't want to be white on Kill Haole day
Made some good buddies Domi, Seu and Glen
I had to get back home, to the rest of my kin
Dad was disappointed, his happiness was down
He knew his son was better suited, in Newtown

NEWTOWN BRED

THIS THING ABOUT US WE ARE NEWTOWN BRED
THE PLACE TO WHERE OUR ANCESTORS FLED
AN AREA WHITE FOLKS USED TO TURN THEIR HEAD
THEY MISSED OUT ON OUR GREATNESS INSTEAD
I WON'T FORGET HOW THEY LOOK DOWN ON US
WE KNEW AT SCHOOL, NOT MANY TO TRUST
THATS WHY I SCREAM MY HOOD WHEN I CAN
PROUD OF THAT PLACE MADE ME A MAN
WATCHED OTHERS EXECUTE THEIR PLANS
OPTIONS FOR COLLEGE, I'M IN POPULAR DEMAND
US THAT LIVED IT, ONLY KNOW HOW GRAND
RUNNING UP TO SAY HELLO TO MR. CAN
OF MR. WADE HARVIN I'M A BIG FAN
THE FRIENDS I MADE IN THAT TIME SPAN
I KNOW THIS DOESN'T NEED TO BE SAID
IF YOU'RE FROM NEWTOWN YOU'RE NEWTOWN BRED
WPC 💪

BAD DUDE

I WAS A BAD DUDE BACK AT THE VIEW
BUT UNFORTUNATELY THEY NEVER THREW
RUNNING THE BALL IS WHAT THEY LIKED TO DO
I WAS A GOOD BLOCKER SO I HANDLED THAT TOO
BUT THERE WERE A FEW TIMES , WHEN WE GOT BEHIND
NOW IT'S THIS KID, YOU WANT TO FIND
I FINALLY REALIZED I WAS PRETTY GOOD, AFTER TAKING ONE 50,
ON FT. PIERCE WESTWOOD
NEEDED POINTS VS. CHAMP MANATEE
BUSTED ONE ON THEM AND THE DEFENSIVE MVP
FOR DEFENSES, I WAS A MISMATCH
OPEN ENOUGH TO AVERAGE 27 A CATCH
IT WAS ONLY 11 CATCHES
BUT THEY GOT THAT WORK IN BATCHES
I'M THANKFUL FOR COACH AND ALL THE FUN
BUT I BELIEVE HAD HE THROWN THE BALL MORE WE'D HAVE WON.

MET MICHAEL JORDAN

I MET MICHEAL JORDAN ON MY TRIP TO UNC,
I JUST COULDN'T BELIEVE IT, IT WAS ETHAN, MJ AND ME
ETHAN HORTON WAS A STAR AND ALSO WAS MY HOST
YOU MUST BE A BAD DUDE HE SAYS WITH A BOAST
NORMALLY I DON'T FOOL WITH, NO RECRUITS
BUT YOU'RE ONE OF THEIR, BIG PURSUITS
THE WOMEN WERE PRETTY, THERE WERE A SLEW
RAN INTO MJ WALKING TO CURFEW
THE INTRODUCTION WAS VERY COOL AND ALL
MJ ASKED CAN I PLAY BALL
I TOLD HIM I'M JUST AS GOOD AS YOU
JUST A DIFFERENT SPORT AND SHOE
HE LAUGHED AND WALKED AWAY
TURNED AND STATED, WE'LL SEE SOMEDAY
I THANKED ETHAN FOR BEING SO KIND
AND BOY OH BOY WE HAD A GOOD TIME

Best Athlete

NOBODY THAT LEAVES THEIR HOMETOWN IS THE BEST
THERE'S ALWAYS A BETTER ATHLETE STUCK HOME IN SOME MESS
EVERY CITY HAS A FABLED HOMETOWN HERO
COULDN'T GO TO COLLEGE, THEIR GPA WAS ZERO
OR HE HAD GAME, THAT WAS EXTREMELY LARGE
POLICE WAITING OUTSIDE, WITH A CHARGE
IT TAKES MORE THAN ATHLETICS, TO GET YOU OUT
YOUR GRADES AND CHARACTER MUST BE STOUT
COLLEGES WILL SEND IN THEIR BEST SCOUT
SO WATCH WHO YOU HANG WITH AND RUN THE RIGHT ROUTES
YOU THINK YOU'RE A MAN CARRYING THAT CHROME
THAT'S THE ATTITUDE THAT KEEPS YOU HOME

MAN ABOUT A MULE

My grandfather was a man that kept his cool
I asked him where he's going,
To see a man about a mule
It was a nice way of saying it's not for you to know
Don't concern yourself where I'm bout to go
Over time I knew his rule
I wasn't gonna play with Jewell
He knew his grandson was a fool
Where you going down to the school
I knew... A man about a mule

ORIGINAL

Js

Converse had a shoe for Dr. J
Owned 2 pair, 1 for school and 1 to play
I loved those shoes, they made me rise
They looked good too, and came in my size
Wore them with outfits, knew I was fresh
With just about all of my clothes, they meshed
As you can see, this shoe had my support
Taking dudes to the hoop on the BBall court
When I hear the kids speak these days
That they're going to get some J's
That's not what my mind portrays
Converse should go do surveys
To gauge interest to replay
And bring back the Original Js

Against The Grain

I HAD TO GO AGAINST MY FAMILY WHEN DECIDING ON A SCHOOL
MY MOTHER WENT TO FAMU, SAID FSU WASN'T COOL
SHE COULDN'T GO ON THAT SIDE OF THE STREET
SHE WAS THERE DURING THE SIT-INS BLACK FOLKS WERE BEAT
THEY ALL WANTED ME TO GO TO UGA
TOLD HER, BET THEY WERE RACISTS IN THEIR DAY
I'M THE ONE THAT HAS TO GO THERE AND STAY
THEY RESPECTED WHAT I DID SAY
MAKING MY DECISION FELT REALLY GOOD
I WAS BEGINNING TO STEP INTO ADULTHOOD

GET SOMETHING FROM THEM

AS I'M PREPARING TO HEAD OFF TO COLLEGE
GRANDMA WANTED TO SHARE SOME OF HER KNOWLEDGE
I EXPECT YOU GO THERE AND FINISH SCHOOL
ANYTHING LESS I WILL NOT APPROVE
PLAYING FOOTBALL IS WHAT THEY WANT TO EXTRACT
I WANT YOU TO GRADUATE AND GET SOMETHING BACK
SHE DIED AND UNFORTUNATELY, DIDN'T GET TO SEE
AFTER 2 NFL OFF-SEASONS, I HAD MY BACHELOR'S DEGREE
I'M SO GLAD WE ENTERED THAT PACT
I'M NOT SURE, I'D HAVE GONE BACK
I'M TRULY THANKFUL TO HER FOR THAT

THANK GOD I COULD PRODUCE

MY HS COACH JOHN SPRAGUE COULD JUICE

WHAT I MEAN IS HE COULD PROMOTE

THE COLLEGE COACHES CAME & TOOK NOTE

HE TAUGHT ME HOW TO WORK HARD EARLY

HIS PRACTICES WERE INTENSE AND BURLY

NOT CATCHING PASSES FULL OF FRUSTRATION

STILL WAS ONE OF THE TOP IN THE NATION

HE WANTED ME TO ATTEND UGA, NOT IN GOD'S PLANS

MAY HE REST EASY NOW, IN GOD'S HANDS

COACH SPRAGUE

COACH WARD

COACH WARD HAS BEEN VERY PIVOTAL TO ME
WITHOUT HIM I'M NOT SURE WHERE I'D BE
10TH GRADE THOUGHT I WAS A HOOPER
COACH TOLD ME FOOTBALL WAS MY FUTURE
BY 12TH GRADE HE WAS EXTREMELY RIGHT
I COULD GO TO ANY SCHOOL THAT I'D LIKE
HE PULLED ME TO THE SIDE HE HAD HEARD
THAT I WAS NOT HONORING MY WORD
COMMITTED TO GEORGIA, WANTED TO CONCENTRATE
I HAD ONE MORE TRIP TO FLORIDA STATE
THE TRIP SHOWED THEY WEREN'T THE SAME
THANKS TO HIM, I'M IN THE FSU'S HALL OF FAME

High School All-Star Game

STATE OF FLORIDA USED TO HAVE AN ALL STAR GAME
NORTH AGAINST SOUTH IT'S NO LONGER THE SAME
THE YEAR I PLAYED, THE NORTH TOOK SOME LICKS
THE SOUTH WAS FULL OF 1ST AND 2ND ROUND PICKS
CHOSEN FOR THE GAME I WAS HAPPY TO BE
TRACEY SANDERS THREW ME, THE FIRST TD
MICHAEL IRVIN SAID HE WANTED TO HAVE FUN
SO THEY THREW HIM A PASS THEN HE SCORED ONE
CAREFREE, WE WERE SUCH MERRY MEN
NEXT TD WAS CAUGHT BY BRETT PERRIMAN
THE NORTH TRIED TO PUT UP A FIGHT
BUT THAT WAS SHUT DOWN BY LORENZO WHITE
A SQUAD LIKE THIS WAS REALLY SCARY
AND WE GOT MORE POINTS FROM CLEVELAND GARY
WE HAD A REAL AWESOME TEAM
ANY FOOTBALL COACH'S DREAM

4 YEAR STARTER

Not many can say, in their college day
I started all 4 years, on their resume'
Left the (941) with nothing to barter
Wanted to be the MAN, so I had to work harder
Coaches and upper classmen in my way
Only an injury could stifle my play
Shined bright in camp, making a name
But I didn't play a snap, in the 1st game
Contemplated leaving that night like a gypsy
Next day the starter, came to the meeting tipsy
Suspension handed down and so he sat
What he didn't know is, he wasn't getting it back
Played well the rest of my time
And for 3 more years that job was mine
So, what ever you think of Pat Carter
He Left FSU, a 4 year starter

Tracey Sanders

WHEN I SIGNED TO FLORIDA STATE
THEY ASSIGNED A KID FROM PALMETTO AS MY ROOMMATE
WHEN I HEARD THE NEWS I THOUGHT IT WAS FATE
WE'D BOTH GO THERE AND DO GREAT
HE THREW ME THE 1ST TD IN THE HIGH SCHOOL ALL STAR GAME
SO I KNEW WE'D GO TO TALLAHASSEE AND DO THE SAME
A BENEFIT OF HAVING HIM WITH ME IN THE ROOM
HE WAS ALSO A BARBER IF I NEEDED TO BE GROOMED
I WAS THE THE WILD ONE HE WAS ALWAYS QUIET
WHEN THEY CHANGED HIS POSITION I WANTED TO RIOT
SUCH A GREAT ATHLETE HE EASILY MADE THE TRANSITION
HE ADAPTED SMOOTHLY TO HIS NEW POSITION
BUT OFTENTIMES WHEN I DO THINK BACK
I'D HAVE LOVED TO SEEN WHAT HE COULD'VE DONE AT QUARTERBACK

COACH MCDUFFIE GETS THE CREDIT FOR MY DEVELOPMENT
BRAD SCOTT TOO, FOR ALL HIS TIME SPENT
COACH MAC WAS A NO NONSENSE COACH
TECHNICALLY FROM GEORGIA, BY HIM I WAS POACHED
STRONG DISCIPLINARIAN AND BIG ON TECHNIQUE
COACH SCOTT PUSHED ME TO REACH MY PEAK
MAC SAYS CARTER YOU GOTTA BLOCK TO GET ON THE FIELD
HE MUST HAVE FORGOTTEN THAT WAS MY APPEAL
I WAS A PRETTY GOOD PLAYER BY MY SENIOR SEASON
THERE'S NO DOUBT COACH MAC WAS THE REASON

WAYNE MCDUFFIE

John Shaft is my cinematic idol
When I got to college Jamie Dukes had that title
On the field JD was very dominant
I followed his lead and became prominent
Turned on the tape of practice, we review
Great job Jamie, is all the coaches spew
He was an All-American and made several teams
I knew he was a pro, atleast that's how it seems
But the NFL Draft came and went
For Jamie, not one draft pick spent
If he didn't get picked, didn't want to be a fool
Made me really buckle down in school
Jamie's height ended up being the reason
But don't feel for him he played 11 seasons.

Jamie Dukes

BRAD SCOTT!

Coach Scott was my position coach all 4 seasons
My family had a bad taste in their mouth and he was the reason
He came to the house and did something lame
He meant well but he called my grandmother by her 1st name
That's something you don't do in the hood
So initially our start wasn't good
But I got on campus and showed potential
My full development was his essential
He was young then finding his way
Followed McDuffie's lead, echoed what he'd say
I soon became dominant in my play
He is credited with my improved display
And I'm for ever thankful to him to this day

BO JACKSON

I GOT A CALL MIDDLE OF THE WEEK
IT WAS MY GRANDMOTHER, SHE WANTED TO SPEAK
SHE WORRIED ABOUT THE NEXT TEAM WE PLAYED
BO JACKSON AND AUBURN HAD HER AFRAID
YOU COULD HEAR THE CONCERN IN HER VOICE
SHE WAS SCARED BUT IT'S MY CHOICE
"BO JACK" GONNA HURT YOU, SHE REVEALED
WE WON'T BE TOGETHER, ON THE FIELD
SHE THEN ASKED WAS I GOING TO CLASS
I SAID CONFIDENTLY, I'M GONNA PASS
HANGING UP CLOSE TO CURFEW,
SAID BYE, DON'T LET BO JACK HURT YOU

DANNY McMANUS

DANNY MAC

He was my quarterback while at State
He's what made our offense great
He earned my respect when he rebuked
Our best O-Lineman, Jamie Dukes
Right then he was our Chief
Injuries robbed him, like a thief
Senior year he's in the best of health
Which increased the teams success and wealth
The NFL really had some Gall
So He went to Canada and is inducted in their Hall.

FRED JONES

For FSU, Fred and I both played
He's a real wise fella from South Dade
We hit it off well in school
He and Pablo played a trick that's cruel
They put garbage bags on my car seat
Then ran and hid indiscreet
In the dumpster the bags were placed
They jumped out laughing with smiles on their faces
Showed immeasurable strength, when Pablo died
And some of that strength I relied
Had some great times with this guy
Holds me accountable, takes no alibi
Our wives are good friends too
We roll with them where oceans are blue
That's my friend he's tried and true

DEION SANDERS

Love him or hate him, this my friend
I can pick up the phone, his voice on the other end
I've known this dude, since 1985
When he quietly announced, he arrived
Was gonna play baseball, like Hank Aaron
Rolling in his custom, drop top Lebaron
He really, showed me some skill
A beautiful punt return, in Gainesville
Really good hoops player, we all balled
Played in the same division, when the NFL called
Dropped a pass, head around late
Says catch the ball, we Florida State
Proud of him, he's an all time great
God's help, he endured a lot of hate
Rooting for him, Colorado his estate
As long as he's there they'll be my #2
Nobody comes before FSU
One more things that still draws tears
We gonna always bag on each others ears

BOBBY BOWDEN

Bobby Bowden was a very great coach
Some thought him special in his approach
He was a excellent teacher and motivator
Had no problem disciplining violators
Led us through some rough spots
Like when Pablo Lopez was shot
We even reached some team goals
Like playing in a New Years Day Bowl
My senior year he started a new thing
5th year seniors didn't practice spring
When I heard this I was highly upset
I played more than all of those vets
I set up a meeting with coach B
And I don't recall what he said to me
Standing outside his door.... It's the wildest thing...
Coach Bowden had me fired up, ready for spring

RIP Coach

HIGH BROW

I won't call no names

I'm sure he'd be ashamed

He tried to use me, to be seen

Tom Browne Park, bunch of black queens

He was already, playing in the pros

Eventually I'd get there, everyone knows

He tossed his keys, for me to pull up his car

Those keys hit the ground, dude I'm the Star

We can laugh about that now

Fronting on me, I couldn't allow

I don't like to, but I can get high brow

God has since Humbled me, that I avow

MICKEY ANDREWS

Coach Andrews came to FSU my sophomore year in school
He also had a son Ronnie who was really cool (RIP)
Coach Andrews had a drill during Matts
Let's just say we were some tired cats
Became a fan of his very quickly
He was just like McDuffie very prickly
Not to mean any insult
They both expected results
He was a straight shooter and I liked that
We didn't really do a whole Lotta chit chat
He came in and turned that D around
And led the Defense to 2 National Crowns
One more thing about him I think is rare
He was a bad man at Bama playing for Bear.

ALMOST LEFT

1986 season was rough on our soul
Distractions and shortcomings, we're in the Liberty Bowl
Birmingham was where the game was played
One night we were late for curfew to the hotel we stayed
Threatened to send us back to the house
Coaches were mad, punishment was doused
Magdi and I
Two Sararsota guys
I was so glad that we won
That win was a lotta fun
At Bama, Ray Perkins retired
Bobby Bowden is who they wanted to hire
Coach had the big decision he'd always yearned
Opted to stay in N. Florida, a monster team he returned
So glad he he decided to stay in the sun
The following year was the 1st of a 15 year run.

MIAMI GAME

COACH BOWDEN SAID WE'RE GOING FOR 2
MY MIND SAYS IT'S COMING TO YOU
MIAMI GAME OF MY SENIOR SEASON
STATE BRAGGING RIGHTS WERE THE REASON
WE'RE BOTH UNBLEMISHED UP TIL THEN
NEEDED THAT GAME TO MAKE MY RECORD EVEN
EARLY IN THE GAME MY MAN TOLBET BAIN
TALKING TRASH TO ME, BUT I HAD TO ABSTAIN
FOCUSED ON GETTING THIS DUB
HE KNOWS I'LL SEE HIM IN A CLUB
I HAD A GREAT ALL AROUND GAME
HAD BRENT MUSBURGER YELLING MY NAME
NOW FOR THE 2 POINT TRY
THE PLAY WAS DESIGNED FOR DANNY AND I
NORMALLY WE ARE ALWAYS ACUTE
BUT ON THIS PLAY WE DIDN'T EXECUTE
MIAMI ENDS UP BEING THE NATIONAL CHAMP
AND FSU FOOTBALL PLANTED THEIR LEGITIMACY STAMP

Melvin Bratton

Mel Bratton hosted me on my visit to UM
I have truly shared, some great times with him
Although we attended, 2 different schools
I'd hang in Miami, him and Bain were cool
Hanging with them, I could just recline
Told me get what I needed, didn't spend a dime
One visit there, enjoying my vacation
The Deejay welcomes me to S. FL, on their radio station
We walk in a club, some Dolphins standing around,
He nods, and says, the Hurricanes run this town
He's gonna always be my man and that you can stamp
But I'm still disappointed he denied me from being a Champ.

Keith Jackson

I thought I was the best TE in the land

Turned on the Oklahoma game

With the ball in his hand

For years I'd heard his name

But never watched his game

He took a reverse man it was sweet

Long TD to the house, Nebraska they defeat

Denied me from reaching my dream

Had to settle for 2nd team

Cool brother too on top of all that

From time to time we still chat

1988
NFL DRAFT

After my college eligibility was complete
I was ready to move to Big Boy Street
I thought I'd go in the 1st round
A couple team were interested, so I found
But after the Patriots, Rams and Bears all picked
I began to panic
But thankful the Lions called at 32
Told me, we're gonna draft you
Happy to get off that board
And I truly thanked the Lord
Sad I didn't get picked by the Rams
A year later Detroit says scram
It's a testament to how God works things out
So good... that He leaves no doubt

Lions 1988 Draft Class

Bennie Blades was the 3rd pick in the draft
Chris Spielman was 29th, far from the aft
I was 32nd, fell down the draft that day
William White was 4th round, With Chris in college he played
I mention all this, for a specific reason
All four of us played atleast 10 NFL seasons
Eric Andolsek was the best of our class
Killed by a truck run over in a crash
I was glad, they traded me away
I preferred natural grass as the surface to play
Unfortunately now, only 3 of us remain,
William is with the Lord, surely heaven's gain.

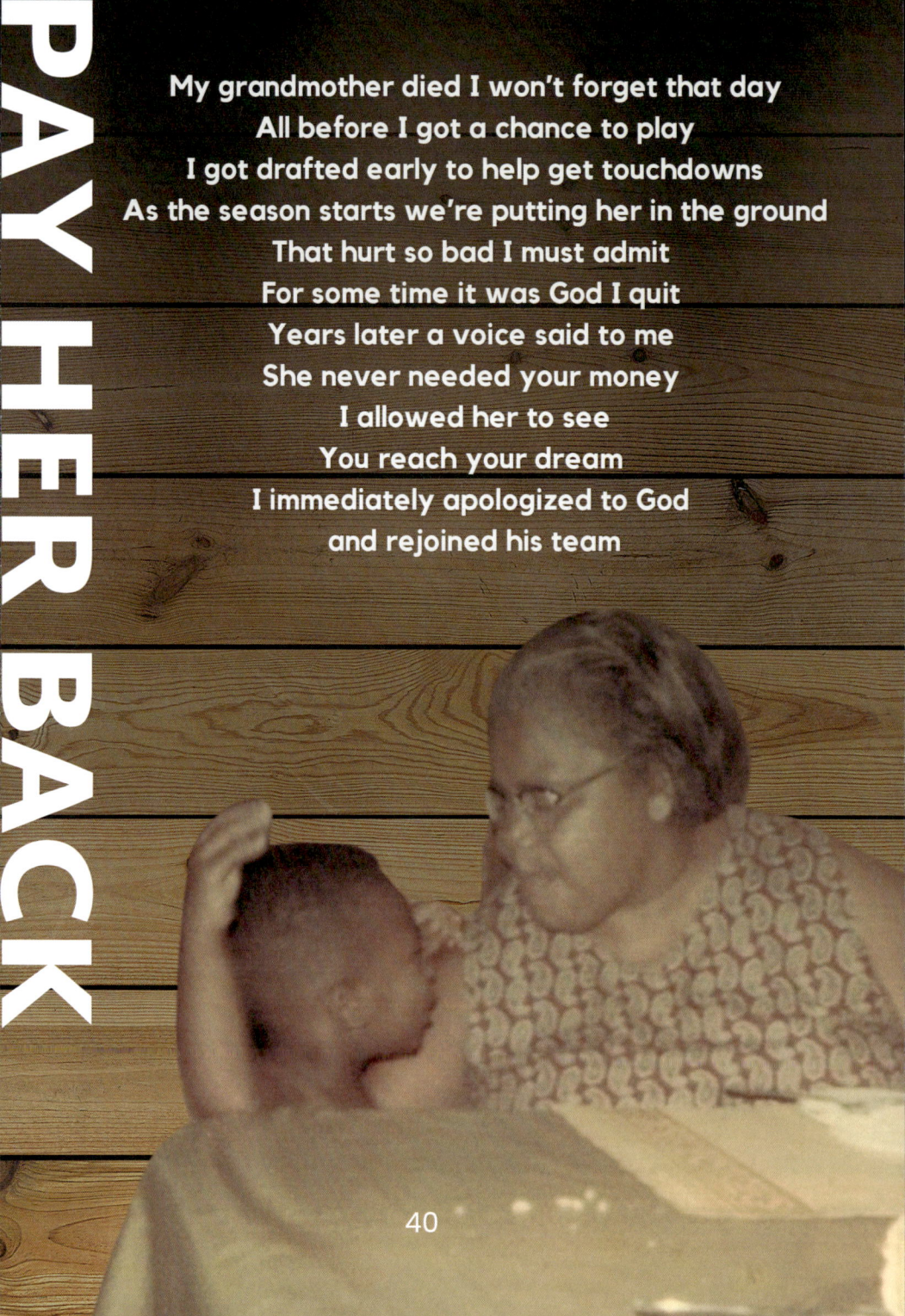

PAY HER BACK

My grandmother died I won't forget that day
All before I got a chance to play
I got drafted early to help get touchdowns
As the season starts we're putting her in the ground
That hurt so bad I must admit
For some time it was God I quit
Years later a voice said to me
She never needed your money
I allowed her to see
You reach your dream
I immediately apologized to God
and rejoined his team

Snow Fall

LIVING IN MICHIGAN, 22 YEARS OLD

FLORIDA MOST MY LIFE, THIS WEATHER'S COLD

WENT TO BED, DIDN'T HEAR A SOUND

WOKE UP TO FRESH SNOW ON THE GROUND

BENNIE AND I HAD NEVER SEEN FRESH SNOW

RAN OUT THE HOUSE, MADE BALLS TO THROW

WILLIAM CAME OUT THE HOUSE LAUGHING AT US

WE DIDN'T CARE AT ALL, WITH SNOWBALLS WE BUST

HERE WE WERE GROWN BEHIND MEN ACTING LIKE WE'RE 10

AND I'D DO IT ALL AGAIN.

YOU CAN'T PLAY

My head coach was fired, my rookie year
Wayne Fontes took over, and made it very clear
They were installing the Run and Shoot
It was a non traditional offense and no TE to boot
Charlie Sanders told Wayne to let that kid go
Allow him to play elsewhere and so his game would grow
I hated that organization, during that era
Front office was rocky, mountainous like the Sierras
The Lions had a scout, his name was Ron Hughes
And I respected him, for his opinion and his views
Said, kid you can play
No matter what they say
I'll never forgot that day
Then I was traded to L.A.

LA/ST. LOUIS RAMS

I HAVE NOTHING BUT LOVE FOR THE RAMS AND THE COMMUNITY
THEY WERE THE ONES WHO GAVE ME AN OPPORTUNITY
WHEN THE LIONS DECIDED TO CHANGE OFFENSIVE SCHEME
THEY TRADED ME TO THE RAMS, MY NEW TEAM
I WAS SO HAPPY TO ARRIVE
DESPITE NOT GETTING TO WEAR 85
ECSTATIC ABOUT LEAVING THAT TURF IN THE SILVERDOME
ANAHEIM STADIUM NATURAL GRASS MY NEW HOME
FOR THAT ORGANIZATION I PLAYED 6 YEARS
2004 MIKE MARTZ HIRED ME TO COACH FORMER PEERS
ONE THINGS FOR SURE AND I CAN'T BE BRIBED
WHEN IT COMES TO THE NFL I'M PART OF THE RAMS TRIBE

California

I have nothing but love for the Golden State
El Pollo Loco was a place I ate
Carl's Jr. Dbl Western bacon
Those earthquakes there left me shaken
Them freeways too, ain't no joke
Riverside county was where I awoke
But I hung in LA , just had to see
Chilling in the Palladium, in the VIP
Glan Slam was Prince's club
El Torito was where I went to grub
South Coast Plaza where I shopped
Ontario airport on a plane I'd hop
Knotts Berry and Disney where I'd stop
15 freeway south I avoided the cops
San Diego is the most beautiful place
Walk over to Mexico their culture I embraced
I will admit California was the truth
But it's best enjoyed during your youth

COMEDY ACT THEATRE

Allow me to share a time when I really had some fun
Just traded to LA from the cold to the Sun
Found my self in the Comedy Act Theatre, Robin Harris is the host
When I tell you he clowned me, I bet it was the most.
When i say I was getting cooked Relentless and I was getting took
I ain't gonna lie, he was funny as can be with all his jokes raining on me.
But the brother was cool, came over after the show
We chopped it up a minute, back to Anaheim we go.

Photo by Henry Yep

GOAT FOR THE Day

I was there that day
When my boy Flipper put on an a display
There's an NFL record that he still holds
336 yards in a game, fella was cold
There were times, Jim just threw it up
Flip went and got it, he was trying to sup
Years later Calvin Johnson struck some fear
There was a game, when he got very near
Thank goodness the clock ran down
Or Flip would have lost his crown
But for all the great receivers to ever play
Flipper is the greatest for a day

FOOTBALL CAMP

I lived in California gave Tim Johnson a call,
He's from Sararsota and he also played pro ball
Was hoping he'd join me doing a camp back home
We came to an agreement to do it, over the phone
We both thought it important to give back
But I wanted to make sure it stayed black
Offers were made for us to move grounds
I wasn't having any of that sound
Everyone was welcomed from all around
But this event here was strictly held in Newtown
Rev John Davis spearheaded the event
Printed tees, ordered food, set up tents
We both had messages to the kids we conveyed
And we did it most of the 90s decade
One more thing the blew my mind
Those Tees were worn in the hood a long time

JACKIE SLATER

I had the honor of playing next to an all time great

He played offensive tackle and attended Jackson State

We had some really good times

Playing together on the Rams O-Line

He's responsible for getting me knocked flat

When he tipped off a defender and yelled come on down Pat

He played an incredible 20 seasons

Which cemented the reason

That he made the Hall of Fame

My Boy Jackie one of the Greats of the Game

Photo by Henry Yep

Magic Johnson's House

I once visited Magic Johnson's house
Just before he had a spouse
And pre-revelation of his sickness
There were women there with thickness
He was hosting a party by the pool
So many celebrities, I thought that was cool
The reason I got in
Was my teammate D Hen
He and Magic were friends
So let the party begin
They had a bikini contest that ended in a tie
1 was in a bathing suit, the other nude, no lie
There were helicopters that someone hired
Come to find out it's the National Enquire
Pics of the party on the cover
Glad they missed me, while they hovered
I had a wonderful time that day
Let's just say....I love L.A.

Marcus Allen

MARCUS ALLEN IS MY FAVORITE BACK OF ALL TIME
I DIDN'T SAY HE'S THE GREATEST, BUT HE'S MINE
HE COULD PRODUCE WHEN HIS NUMBER WAS CALLED
I WATCHED HIM MAKE MANY DEFENDERS FALL
UNSELFISH ENOUGH TO LEAD BLOCK
EVEN WHEN AL DAVIS CONTINUED TO MOCK
STILL LEFT D. COORDINATORS IN SHOCK
MY MAN USED TO TOTE THAT ROCK
I ADMIRED HIS MANY ABILITIES
AND IT INCLUDED HIS VERSATILITY
HE'S IN HALL OF FAME
SMOOTH PLAYER... I ADMIRED HIS GAME

FRONT ROW SEAT

Joe Montana broke my heart
Jerry Rice also did his part
Flew to the bottom, played against Marino
Saw Anthony Munoz, a bad Latino
Peeped OJ… Anderson that is
Eyed Randall Cunningham doing his biz
Thurman Thomas was nasty I must say
I also enjoyed watching Emmitt Smith play
Mike Singletary hit me as a rook
Watched Henry Ellard, DBs he shook
Barry Sanders made defenders fall
Sterling Sharpe was smooth catching that ball
I thought a lot of folks hated
Rickey Watters to me was underrated
A teammate of mine tried to bait Warren Moon,
He'd have been better off sitting in a saloon
This is something I thought I'd share
I saw some bad dudes while up there

Kevin Greene

Kevin Greene was that man
Practiced against him daily and you must have a plan
Great guy to work with, you're gonna improve
If you didn't, you'd have been removed
Every camp we'd battle at that time
His birthday 7-31 a day before mine
I know he made me better and hope I did the same
But it was extremely fun facing him in a game
He's now gone on up to heaven
Rest is Peace Kevin (Greene)

Photo by Henry Yep

Ronnie Lott

Interactions with Ronnie were not a lot
But let me tell of a few of our shots
On the goal line he sliced off the edge
He could bring that heat, it's not alleged
With a DB in the box, MAJORITY of the time,
The advantage was all mine
To describe to you... that he's great
Good enough to cause a stalemate
260 lbs coming at you, and I brought wood
I didn't dominate enough of those, like I should.

Chicken And Waffles

WHEN I GOT TO CALIFORNIA FROM WHERE IT SNOWS
MY TEAMMATE D HEN ASKED HAD I HEARD OF ROSCOES
THEY SERVE CHICKEN AND WAFFLES AS A DISH
THEY DON'T GO TOGETHER, AIN'T NO WAY, THEY WISH
HE TAKES ME TO THIS NOW FAMOUS PLACE
AFTER THAT 1ST BITE, HE LAUGHS IN MY FACE
KNEW I WAS SUCKED ALL THE WAY IN
INTRODUCED ME TO THE OWNERS, SAYS HE'LL BE HERE AGAIN
JUST AS HE PREDICTED
I BECAME ADDICTED
SOON REALIZED I HAD TO STOP THAT DATE
THE RAMS HAD A CLAUSE ON MY WEIGHT

TERRY CREWS

Permit me to tell you about Terry Crews
In practice he was bad news
He was a young fella trying to make his way
Everyday in practice, he was blowing up a play
He played hard, so it wasn't malicious
But this fella, could be really vicious
Years later when he was on the screen
My kids were little & said something mean
Hey my man Terry Crews
You don't know him they accuse
No matter what I said they still refused
But, As they grew of age
They realized we shared the same stage
After I watched his movie White Chicks
That brother had me transfixed
As a late round pick he was always stressing
Look at him now, basking in God's Blessings

GAME DAY 1

When I was a backup, you know what was real
Game Day for me, was on that practice field
The defense was gonna get this smoke
I was hungry to play, the desire remained stoked
Although I was unhappy, I stayed on top of my craft
Start of every new year, there's a new face from the draft
They always attempt to push the youth
You better have game when you're long in the tooth.
If you're a backup and want to play
Make every practice your Game Day.

Chuck was my favorite coach

He was also old school, didn't mind reproach

He'd let you have it, so you knew where you stood

He also gave praise to those he should

Gave me a chance when thought a malcontent

I was the starter the rest of my extent

Hired Mike Martz to coach the tight ends

Mike understood, in me he could depend

If you know Chuck he had a lot isms

He also brought to us his wisdom

So glad he came to Rams Park

A few of us guys needed his spark

For 2 seasons I got to shine

Thanks to Coach Knox coming to Anaheim

CHUCK KNOX

 MIKE MARTZ

There's a man I admire very much
As time has grown we've lost touch
He has been a blessing since we met
Coached me and molded a vet
Later gave me a job on his staff
Shared some good times and laughs
Gave me insight on his approach
I'm forever grateful to Coach.

CREATURE
OF HABIT

Most folks don't like change
Attempting it can feel strange
Let me tell you about an event
Where a little change made a Dent
By this time I'm a 5 year vet
New coaching staff, the starting job gonna get
Coach Martz wanted me to change my stance
I was resistant, but I took a chance
It gave me an advantage, even my game enhanced
And it also assisted my career to advance
That also helps the finance
All because I took a chance

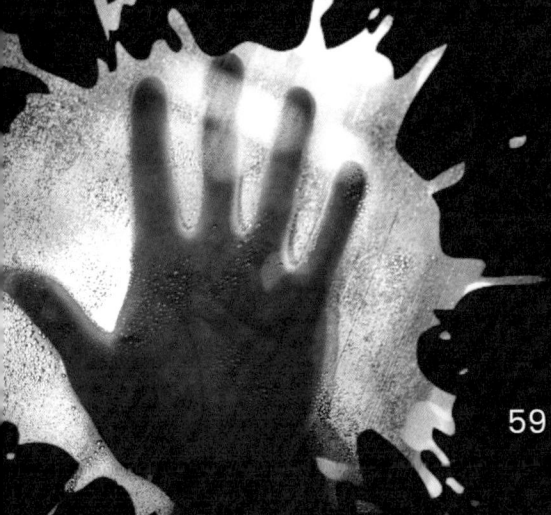

20 POINT DOG

IN 1992 WE WERE A 20 POINT DOG
SAYING THAT WE'RE SORRY, LIKE A BUMP ON A LOG
WE WERE UP AGAINST THE EVENTUAL CHAMPION DALLAS COWBOYS
A SUPER TEAM OF PLAYERS WITH ALL THEIR TOYS
CHUCK TOLD US TO GO OUT AND KEEP OUR POISE
IN TEXAS STADIUM AMONG ALL THAT NOISE
THEN IT WAS CLEVELAND GARY WHO ZAMPESE DEPLOYS
HENRY AND FLIPPER DALLAS DBS THEY DESTROY
YOU COULD SEE IT ON HIS FACE COACH WAS OVERJOYED
I CAUGHT A FEW PASSES IN THEIR VOIDS
IRVIN DIDN'T WANT TO SPEAK AFTER, HE WAS ANNOYED
THE W ON THIS DAY THE RAMS ENJOYED.

Angry At a Blessing

High school or college I never rode the pine
Thankful I was just good enough to get a lil shine
Rookie year I'm a starting, in the Silverdome
Traded to LA, William White called my home
Not playing a lot for 3 years, I was an unhappy young man
Wrapped up in myself, not realizing God's plan
Those years that I did not play
Kept me healthy enough to stay
All the while I'm mad, days just expressing
That same thing all the along was a huge blessing

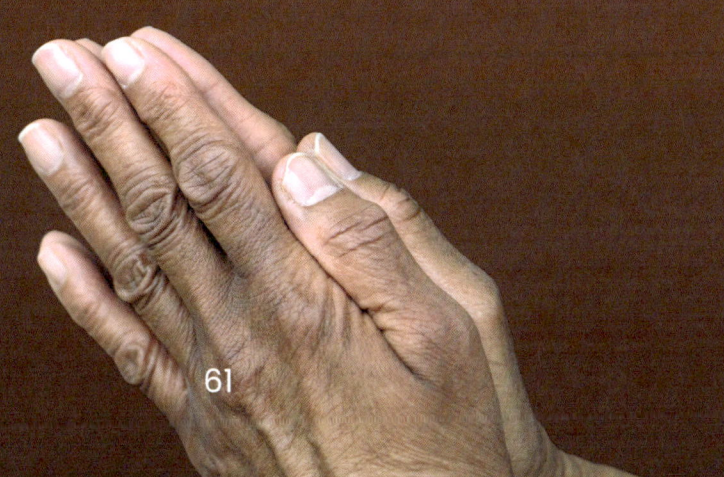

MONSTERS

Don't doubt these boys today ain't peak
During my era, I had a monster every week
One week it's Carl Banks and LT
Next it's Tony Tolbert and Haley
Another guy I could not avoid
#95 for the Steelers LB Greg Lloyd
Never a week off, always top billing
Here's Rickey Jackson and Pat Swilling
As a TE these matchups were chilling
These dude came thru filling
Thought I escaped, nope, still in a fight
Here comes Clyde Simmons, Seth and Reggie White
Cornelius Bennett was bad dude, that added a gift
Under that wrapping is Bruce Smith
There's another tandem I can't ignore
Kevin Greene and Lamar Lathon were gonna roar
There's also Derrick Thomas
All Monsters like I promised

BUCS STADIUM

Growing up in the Bay
I used to say
I was going to play
In Bucs stadium one day
I'm on the Rams and we come to town
3-27 at the half, we were way down
But when we started the 2nd half
The Bucs fans all continued to laughed
Their celebration was out of order
We rallied to win in the 4th quarter
The Rams turned those laughs to frowns
The winning TD, a kid from Newtown

JEROME BETTIS

He came to the Rams in the 1st Round

Perfect for Coach Knox and his Ground and Pound

At first sight, He looked pudgy for a back

But I was impressed how he'd find the right crack

But one night in New Orleans vs a D that's stacked

He rushed for over 200 on that D that's all-black

Have to give credit if I got him on the corner

Tim Lester cleaned up and JBs a goner

Jerome had a style that was quite unique

He could run with power or shake you with his feet

The Rams to traded him to Three Rivers

Where throughout his career he delivers

Got him a ring before he left the game

Then 2015 a call from the Hall of Fame

Though he's my guy I still hate Notre Dame

But he was a bad dude ain't no shame. 💯

Photo by Henry Yep

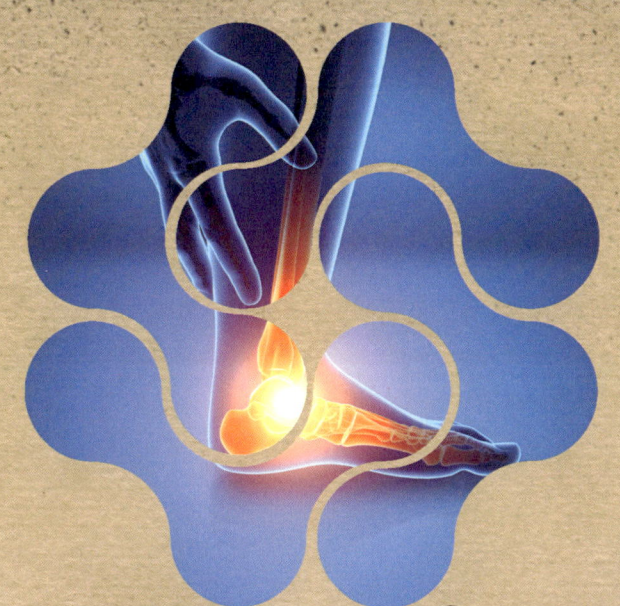

Sprained My Foot

In High school, college and the 1st 5 years
No injury had stopped me playing against my peers
But at the very start of 1993
Had my very 1st injury
The shoe collapsed under my foot
A foot sprain is how it's put
6 weeks sidelined to heal
Troy Drayton went on to appeal
Come back I'm never the same
But thankful to continue playing the game.

MIND MY BUSINESS

Let me tell you about a time
When the NFL sent me a fine
They really made me whine
But they had opined
A teammate and defender were intertwined
Also they had blows combined
I only stepped in to unwind
But damages to me were assigned
Afterwards...only my business I mind

HOUSTON
OILERS

Man what a talented bunch of men
But that front office you couldn't depend
Enticed me there to play with Warren Moon
Immediately heard he was traded one afternoon
Some good brothers there like Bubba, Lo White and Mark Rob
Slaughter, Wood and EG an easy QB job
Coach got fired middle of the year
Fisher took over and to him we'd adhere
Training camp 95, his office with the door shut
Informed me that I was getting cut
And as soon as they did the Rams picked me up

WELCOME TO H-TOWN

I had just move to Houston in a hotel on S. Main
The only thing about city, that I can complain
I just finished working out, then back to the room
Never happened before, but it caused me gloom
Someone stole my car on a whim
Funny cause Alonzo said it happened to him
Insurance paid full, no need to frown
Guess this was my Welcome to H-Town

HOUSTON CELEBS

The folks in Houston were really cool
I attended many parties outside by the pool
A game of Spades with Carl Lewis I'd play
Met Warren Moon, but they traded him away
At Lo White's party I met Moses Malone
Visited Leroy Burrell at his home
Scarface was cool, had him flustered
Took his money, shooting hoops at Dave & Busters
Met Lil Troy at a golf event
I loved their southern accent
There are many more can't remember all
While living there I had a ball
Loved that Galleria Mall
But all of that now is past
But some memories last

BLACK COWBOYS

I have no idea why I showed
As I'm riding down Almeda road
To pull over into a horses stable
Got out sat at the table
Made my presence known
Then we played some bones
Black Cowboys didn't know they existed
In my history book they're not listed
Filled me in on the perspective of their history
Made me understand why they were a mystery
Invited my kids to come on out
Their horse needed a workout
That was a great place to dwell
And I pray those fellas doing well

Bruce Matthews

I have been around some greats
And Bruce Matthews is one of their mates
An incredible talent can play anywhere on the OLine
And was bad enough to also whip your behind
Big man impressed handling the ball playing hoops
Superbly for his size group
Bruce played 20 years at a high level
Beat him playing chess and I got to revel
I played against his brother Clay
He should be in the Hall with Bruce someday

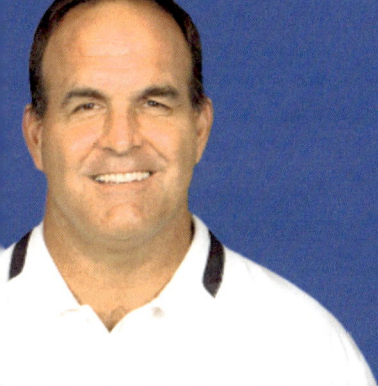

DUI

My ex said boy ALRIGHT
You know you just got off a flight
I should have just heeded
Jammed up in something, not needed
In south Florida visiting mother in law
Also An opportunity to feed my flaw
I really wanted to see friends at the club
She told me to eat, I didn't want to grub
Went out and had drinks that night
Police tapping on the window, I was asleep at a light
Arrested, booked, placed in jail
Broward county police saved my tail
My ID and info was sent to my castle
Prevented the media from giving me a hassle
News say, Wendell Carter takes a fall
Nobody knew who that was at all
Those 8 hours in went by like a snail
Gloria Jean Smith came thru and paid my bail ♥

CARLOS JONES

People enter your life for only a season
God puts in others for a reason
Growing up I knew Mr. Carlos Jones
He's the guy at the funeral home
In 1994 he told me he'd visit one day
Said when the Oilers and the Steelers play
I've heard that said many times before
But he called and told me he was walking out the doo
He was in the Astrodome to my surprise
We lost the game but I found him wise
Shared things with me that opened my eyes
Made me accountable quit the denies
Cool thing about it he was older than me
Shared potential pitfalls I couldn't see
He was a big brother I never had
Preferred talking to him more than my dad
Showed me how to move loudly without making noise
How to deal with others without losing poise
Just as good as a West BBQ Thin End
That's how good a friend he's been

ISAAC BRUCE

IKE IS MY GUY, A REAL GOOD BROTHER
MET HIM IN '95 WHEN DBS COULDN'T COVER
HE'S MAD, BECAUSE HE KNEW HE WAS GREAT
THAT BOBBY BOWDEN DIDN'T CALL HIM TO STATE
I'M PROUD OF DUDE AND HOW HIS CAREER CONCLUDED
MADE THE HALL OF FAME, TOO SIGNIFICANT TO BE EXCLUDED
HE'S A FLORIDA BOY, THAT GOD HAS EMPOWERED
FROM DILLARD HIGH SCHOOL, IN THE HEART OF BROWARD
HE'S LEADING FOLKS TO GOD, AND HIS FAITH WILL NEVER END
MAKES SENSE NOW, WHY THEY CALLED HIM THE REVEREND

KEVIN CARTER

Allow me to take you back to 1995
Cut by the Oilers to St. Louis I arrive
Kevin Carter was the number 1 pick of the team
I'm an old vet and he was finding his way it seemed
He's from the capital city in the Sunshine State
Said we were cousins, he told High School mates
I knew he'd be good once he put it together
This young fella could bring that leather
Next year I'm in Arizona with the Rams coming to town
Carter vs. Carter NFL Showdown
I have to admit he put it on me that day
Never seen someone improve so drastically in their play
10 years later I'm coaching tight ends
I tell my players that we're some kin

BAPTIZED IN THE SHOWER

1995 was a tough year in my life
Full blown Alcoholic and trouble with my wife
The trouble was all on me,
loved sipping Long Island iced teas
A group of fellas on my St. Louis squad
Met and talked about God
I sat in one, guilt provoked
Spoke with Big Sean and Fred Stokes
Both men flawed, but pretty wise
Convinced me the need to get baptized
Reminded me, that I needed God's power
They baptized me in the locker room shower
So glad I decided to obey
It put me where I am today
I'm still thankful for those men
God's goodness Shined thru in the end

ARIZONA CARDINALS

As 1996 free agency rolls around
The Arizona Cardinals invited me to town
It was year 9, and I got down
It was me, who Boomer Esiason found
Simeon Rice was a rookie that year
Aeneas Williams All-Pro abilities stood clear
Erics Swann and Hill were there to fear
There was a game that season we had regrets
Losing to the winless Jets
My engine was on full throttle
The last season I struggled with that bottle
I really enjoyed playing with those men
And they brought me back for year ten.

LARRY CENTERS

Hopes he makes the Hall of Fame

I'm so Happy he got a rang

He was my teammate for a 2 years

Dude really could ball, loved him catching fleers

Could catch as well as any one on the field

I really liked his game and he played with zeal

Off the field he was real cool

Tried to hustle me playing pool

He was the type of player that would run thru a wall

I really hopes he hears from the Hall

SIMON SHANKS

I know a guy, I owe many thanks
He was my teammate in Arizona
his name was Simon Shanks
I take you back to 1996
When alcohol and me just didn't mix
I'm in the club causing a mess
He stepped in during my duress
I think he was polite, maybe said please
But he stepped up to me, and took away my keys
I'm certain, I wouldn't have slept in my bed
He truly saved me from jail or being dead
Years later, I hear he left his kids and wife
All because someone decided to take his life
Sad to hear about his death
I'll always owe him til my last breath
28 years later I'm still giving thanks
And that's why I'll never forget Simon Shanks

TITO/TITOYA

I once had a teammate name Tito
Back when I drank mojitos
We used to banter back and forth
He's a Florida boy that went to college up north
One day our banter took a turn
He thought he'd made a slick burn
Says OK, Patricia is the name of my sister
I said, my sibling named Titoya mister
The plane all laughed He had doubt
We all laughed hard throughout
He decided to eat his meal
And having a sister named Titoya was real.

ALCOHOL ISN'T YOUR FRIEND

Alcohol has caused countless deaths
So many innocent lives, so many last breaths
Alcohol will never be your friend
It will always let you down in the end
You may think it's cool, so you befriend
Slippery enough to make you depend
That's what the devil did intend
Prayers is what I had to send
Grace is what God extends
Another wound God had to mend

Mean Joe Green

Coach Greene was alright
He didn't talk much at first sight
He coached D-Line on the Cards
He mean mugged and always looked hard
But when he seen I could play a tad
He warmed a little and wasn't so bad
Here I was an 8 year pro
Playing fan boy to Mean Joe 😁

THE PROGRAM

I have to give credit to the League
Plus the fact that I was getting fatigued
They helped me break alcohol's grip
Tested to make sure I didn't slip
Directed me to the right support
They held me accountable and blocked my attempt to abort
FOREVER THANKFUL for stepping in during my need
I'm a player from THE PROGRAM and so thankful…indeed. 🙏🏾

BRO. LANCE

Bro. Lance let me tell you bout my dude
He's an elder in the community that cooks good food
Always sharing wisdom and encouragement
I once hired him to cater his nourishment
I'm on the Cardinals we coming to town
Bragged to all the fellas how he got down
The Bucs game was over looking for him in the parking lot
He was no where to be found in the spot
Bus pulls off disappointment begins
Pull up on the tarmac I had a huge grin
I had to double check eyes and strain
Saw Bro Lance was walking off the plane
His garlic crabs were the toast on the ride back home
I respect him so much is why I write this poem

SUN DEVIL
STADIUM

IF YOU PLAYED SPORTS, I HOPE YOU HAD FUN
THERE WILL BE A TIME YOU PLAY YOUR LAST ONE
SENIOR YEAR IN COLLEGE WE'RE IN THE FIESTA BOWL
BEAT NEBRASKA FINISHED 2 IN THE POLLS
FAST FORWARD 10 YEARS LATER
WITH LOMAS BROWN A DECORATED GATOR
I'M IN THE NFL AND IT'S YEAR TEN
MY FOOTBALL CAREER WAS AT THE END
WE PLAYED THE ATLANTA FALCONS IN TEMPE
THAT WAS THE VERY LAST GAME FOR ME
IN COLLEGE OR PRO ONE THING IS THE SAME
IN SUN DEVIL STADIUM I PLAYED MY LAST GAME

TIGHT ENDS

80's and 90's

Growing up Kellen Winslow topped my list
Dave Casper was the original Genesis
Jimmie Giles I met when he came to Bucs Day
Doug used to feed him, without any delay
Then I loved Mark Bavaro's game
He could catch and block, I did the same
Steve Jordan was a perennial All-Pro
Brent Jones I envied, because he had Joe
Jay Novacek was quiet or atleast seemed coy
On the field, a great receiving target for Troy
A sneaky bad dude this aint no rumor
Was Rodney Holman catching passes from Boomer
Ferrell Edmonds made the Pro Bowl proud of him
Jackie Harris was a bad dude that stayed in the gym
There are a few dudes I'd never knock
Ethan, Buck and Glove, came in and got the rock
Keith Jackson arrived, he was tough to handle
Setting rookie records, catching passes from Randall
Eric Green doing it at 280 and not fat
Ben Coates was a bad fella and my frat
Shannon Sharpe talked trash but backed it with his play
An excellent option for John Elway
Tony Gonzalez came in, on my way out
Couldn't talk about tight ends and not give a shout

THE LOCKER ROOM

The locker room was a sanctuary for us
A place of sanity that locked out the fuss
The locker room provided solace from outside mess
It was a great place to be to chill and de-stress
In a corner theres always someone rambling
In the other theres a few that are gambling
That place was ours and ours alone
Some talked in their lockers on their phone
Some shared God's word to a few
And there was always something there to chew
But it was always the best place to be, if you enjoyed comedy
Some have music with a little boom
Also was a place we'd get groomed
You need a place to escape gloom
Safest place was the Locker Room

NFL COACHING

I'M FOREVER INDEBTED TO MIKE MARTZ
HE WAS MY COACH AND RECOGNIZED MY SMARTS
HE TOOK A CHANCE ON ME
AND GAVE ME AN OPPORTUNITY
I WAS IN ST. LOUIS WITH HIM, HIS LAST 2 SEASONS
HE TOOK ME TO DETROIT AS HE REASONED
COACHING IS A REALLY TOUGH JOB
YOU DON'T KEEP IT, IF YOUR PLAYER IS A SLOB
THANKS MARRINELLI AND MATT MILLEN
CITY OF DETROIT WAS CHILLIN
I MET REALLY GOOD GUYS ALONG THIS ROAD
GLAD I CAN RECALL THIS WHILE IN MY ABODE

WILBERT MONTGOMERY

I met Will, while coaching with Mike
A very smart fella, and that I liked
Good brother, that always looked out
Showed me what, the biz is about
Helped me, overcome some doubt
In 2008, he and Mike broke out
Over the years, we've stayed in touch
He also helped, my pockets and such
Whenever we eat lunch, it'll never be Dutch
That's my man and he means that much

TORRY
HOLT

This dude had the most amazing hands
Stuff I seen him do was grand
I felt a kinship when he wore 88
I knew he'd end up a great
What made me really like him tho
On Mornings when my energy was low
Walked in meetings had my energy grow
He brought a certain vibe
That brought my excitement alive
I watched him thrive
Worked hard, had great drive
Impressive young dude…
NFL HALL OF FAME …yall being rude

MARSHALL
FAULK

Smart players I absolutely adore
Marshall Faulk is that dude at its core
Knew what everyone was doing on field
Made it easy for his skills to reveal
I had to be to practice but stayed up late
Watching him showout at San Diego State
Real cool guy and I like the way he dressed
But on that field was where he impressed

ORLANDO
PACE

This big dude was smooth
His presence always soothed
He was the anchor of the O-Line
His pass pro was where he Shined
Locked up all pass rushers
Run blocking he's a crusher

No surprise he made the Hall
This big cat could really ball
One more thing I think is funny
Big O if you're reading this I WANT MY MONEY
(UT-USC) 😁

DAN CAMPBELL

In the Late 2000s I Coached in Motown
Not very good team, we were way down
When I was there, Kwame' was the mayor
The team was short on good players
Let me tell you, Dan could ball
He did it at times, One arm and all
There was a kinship we'd agree
He was the same player as me
If I see him I'd never be a snob
He played some good ball and kept me a job
Happy for him and his success in the ranks
I owe him a very big THANKS

CALVIN JOHNSON

I got to witness Calvin Johnson's pro day
There were 2 TEs, there on display
When I tell you Calvin was unreal
He ran a 4.35 that day on the field
6 foot 5 and 230 was his weight
42 inch vertical, he could elevate
The Lions had the 2nd pick overall
He's the baddest prospect, he could ball
He's a guy I knew was a can't miss
I knew some fans would be pissed
The Lions took WRs in their previous 1st Rounds
Guys too good to pass, the table we'd pound
Matt Millen agreed with our call
I'm sure he had a smile, when Calvin made the Hall

LOMAS BROWN

I played with him when I was a rook
Drafted high, thought I'd cook
Good brother, that was also my frat
Traded to LA, had to scat
Linked back up in Tempe for 2
At that time I had issues to work thru
Then 10 years after, same tune
Linked up again, with my man June
I'm on the Lions as a coach
He came to me with a different approach
He set me up on a blind date
Last 15 years, she's been my mate
Whenever I'm in Detroit Downtown
I always holla at Lomas Brown

TONY WYLLIE

Tony Wyllie is my man, I had to put in the book
A real good brother, my back, he looked
He came to the Rams to work for Rick Smith,
for so many of us guys he's been a great gift
A proud graduate of TSU
A humble brother that's a Kappa too
Moved in circles where others dream
Shined so bright behind the scenes
5x Pete Rozelle Award Winner
When we catch up I owe him dinner
Shared some really good laughs with him
Especially the one about Lil Lem
He's the reason I'm a published poet
A powerful guy most folks don't know it
As long as I have breath he's gonna always be my guy
He's a good friend, that I can't deny

David Rocker

I have a very good friend
I say very good...I can depend
Chosen by God to be a leader of men
Has a church in Georgia I'm gonna attend
Throws me scripture to keep me on my toes
Wanting me to succeed greatly shows
A good brother who we both relate
Both played ball so its a level debate
But he keeps me razor edged straight
And to me that makes him GREAT.

NEUROFEEDBACK

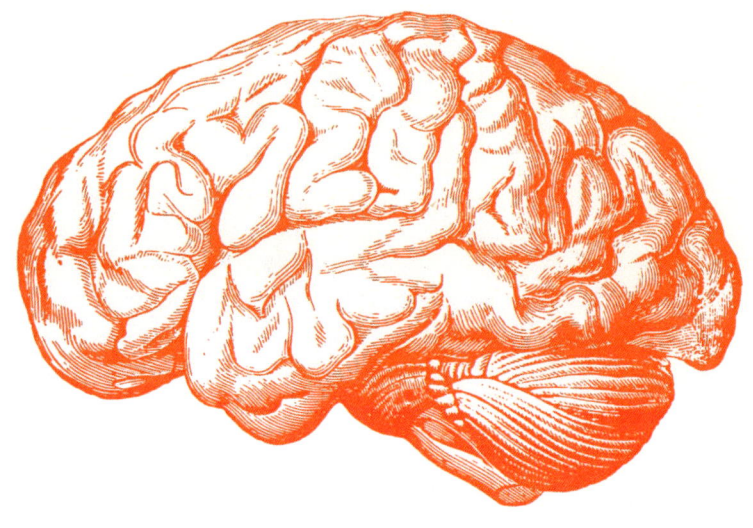

This treatment has been a Godsend
And we can no longer pretend
Former players are having it rough
We anticipated the orthopedic stuff
We missed the damage to our brains
When you're retired the impairment remains
This treatment has saved my life
And also help me keep my wife
There is some irony to explain
These dudes are cousins with the same last name
Dr. George Rozelle is a good practitioner
His cousin Pete. Was the League Commisioner
Pete Rozelle oversaw my draft
George Rozelle saved me with his craft

Mental Health

YOU GOTTA TAKE CARE OF YOUR MENTAL WELL BEING
IF NOT, SADNESS AND SORROW I'M GUARANTEEING
IT'S DELICATE LIKE SHEET GLASS
AND IF YOU DON'T MAINTAIN, IT CAN CRASH
THE BRAIN CAN CREATE THINGS THAT SPARK
IF NOT TREATED PROPERLY CAN TAKE YOU TO THE DARK
THAT'S WHEN YOU FIGHT DEPRESSION
DON'T LIKE IT HERE, I'VE SAID IN CONFESSION
SO NO MATTER HOW MUCH YOU HAVE WEALTH
IT'S PRACTICALLY MEANINGLESS WITH BAD MENTAL HEALTH

HOPE THEY'RE PROUD

I REALLY HOPE THEY'RE PROUD
LOOKING DOWN FROM THE CLOUDS
THAT LITTLE BOY THEY CARED FOR
GOD HAS ALLOWED TO SOAR
HE MADE SOME MISTAKES
THE LORD WAS GRACIOUS AND GAVE HIM BREAKS
YOUR PRAYERS HAVE NOW COVERED HIM 58 YEARS
LONGER THAN A FEW OF HIS PEERS
THE LORD IS NOT DONE WITH HIM, JUST YET
HE'S IN GOOD HANDS, DON'T YOU FRET
HE'S USING ALL THE WISDOM YOU ENDOWED
AND HE'S PRAYING HE MADE YALL PROUD.

MY REQUEST

Are you doing your best

I expect your answer is yes

Are you saving to invest

Out of the streets, getting your rest

Talking to the Lord, sins you confessed

Reading your word with zeal & zest

Those things need to be addressed

You can't be happy stuck in that mess

Don't you dare try to suppress

Now is the time to PROGRESS

Give it to our Creator, my request

100

THE CURRY
COLLABORATIVE

I want to thank my squad for the work behind the scenes,
The Curry Brothers and me—we make a great team.
We're now finishing book number two,
With even more projects we're ready to pursue.

Folks are impressed, they've shared their review,
But I'm just the talent—they let me spew.
No success is gained without what they do,
The Curry Brothers and me are coming for what's due.

PLANTED BY GOD

People asked me where this gift comes from
People who don't believe in Jesus think its dumb
But God gave me this gift
He deposits them I lift
And he's been so far from thrift
Hope my writing makes a diff
My cognitive abilities have declined
I found expression thru rhyme
Poetry has given me a new journey
With an assist from Jesus my attorney
To Worldly folks this may sound odd
Those that know, planted by God.

Got an idea for a book? Contact Curry Brothers Publishing, LLC. We are not satisfied until your publishing dreams come true. We specialize in all genres of books, especially religion, self-help, leadership, family history, poetry, and children's literature. There is an African Proverb that confirms, *"When an elder dies, a library closes."* Be careful who tells your family history. Our staff will navigate you through the entire publishing process, and we take pride in going the extra mile in meeting your publishing goals. Improving the world one book at a time!

Curry Brothers Publishing, LLC
PO Box 247 Haymarket, VA 20168
(719) 466-7518 & (615) 347-9124

Visit us at: www.currybrotherspublishing.com

www.ingramcontent.com/pod-product-compliance
Lightning Source LLC
Chambersburg PA
CBRC091203010526
44107CB00019B/1230